The Complete Slow Cooker Cookbook

Simple Recipes, Extraordinary Results

Table of Contents

BONUS:

As a way of saying thank you for purchasing my book, please use your link below to claim your 3 FREE Cookbooks on Health, Fitness & Dieting Instantly

https://bit.ly/2MLwfjP

You can also share your link with your friends and families whom you think that can benefit from the cookbooks or you can forward them the link as a gift!

Introduction

For many, cooking can be a daunting endeavor. Recipes seem complicated; techniques seem out of reach. It may be quicker to hit the drive through one more night.

A slow cooker recipe, however, takes the fuss out of the kitchen. You control the ingredients to an extent, making the dishes healthy and personalized. The technique is simply pushing a button. Maybe you may have to mix something, and then push a button.

Each recipe in this book embraces the idea of slow cooker simplicity married with delicious and classic flavors. The result is a home cooked meal that cooks itself. Read on to learn how to cook meat and meatless dishes, savory snacks and scrumptious desserts, even drinks and stocks. The convenient yet authentic experience of a slow cooker makes mealtime all the more enjoyable.

Basic Stocks

There is certainly simplicity in buying your chicken, beef, or vegetable stocks from the supermarket. You can choose which brand you'd like and specialize your tastes: low sodium, organic. Throw it in the cart and call it a day.

However, this book is not only about simple meals, but simple meals at not-so-simple quality. While store-bought stocks will do the job, why not spend an extra day at the beginning of the week creating personalized, rich, beautiful stocks that will enhance your meals and also take care of some leftovers you may have? Because you can decide what goes into your stocks and you can control your seasoning, these stocks are much healthier than any you can find in a store. And when we say spend an extra day making stocks, we really mean let your slow cooker spend an extra day making stocks. Simple is the key, after all.

We'll briefly cover a chicken, beef, and vegetable stock that you can substitute for any grocery store stock, and you'll be well on your well to making easy, delicious meals.

Chicken Stock

To save time, use the carcass from a rotisserie chicken for this recipe. Reserve the chicken meat another recipe of your choice.

Ingredients

- 1 rotisserie chicken carcass
- (or carcass from 1 fryer chicken)
- 2 yellow onions (peel and cut into quarter)
- 2 carrots, sliced into 2-inch chunks
- 1 peeled garlic clove
- 2 stalks celery, sliced into 2-inch chunks
- Herbs of your choosing:
- tarragon, bay, thyme, rosemary
- Water to cover carcass (about 3 cups)

Preparation Method:

1. Set all the listed ingredients in your slow cooker and cook on low from 5 to 24 hours.
2. Cook the stock longer if you want it to have a stronger flavor.
3. Using a fine mesh sieve, strain your stock and disregard the vegetables.
4. Store in the refrigerator between uses.
5. Season with a dash of salt and pepper. Yields about 3 cups of stock.

Beef Stock

Your local butcher will have beef bones available. You can put them straight in the slow cooker, but roasting the bones first will add richness to your stock.

Ingredients

- 7-10 beef bones (preferably any with meat still on)
- 2 peeled carrots, sliced into 2-inch chunks
- 2 yellow onions, peeled and quartered
- 2 stalks celery, sliced into 2-inch chunks
- 2 peeled garlic cloves
- 2 Tbsp. dried parsley flakes (optional)
- Water to cover bones (about 3 cups)

Preparation Method:

1. Place bones on a greased baking sheet and roast at 350F for 20 minutes.
2. Turn the bones over, roast for an additional 20 minutes.
3. Place bones in the slow cooker, add all other ingredients, and cook on low from 12 to 24 hours.
4. Remove the bones and veggies – use the mesh to help you out with this.
5. Add flavor by adding salt and spice it up with additional pepper.
6. Store in the refrigerator between uses. Yields about 3 cups of stock.

Vegetable Stock

Adding the parmesan rinds is optional, but it adds a meaty, salty quality that tastes like you added chicken to the stock.

Ingredients

- 2 yellow onions, peeled and quartered
- 3 peeled carrots, sliced into 2-inch chunks
- 1 peeled garlic clove
- 3 stalks celery, sliced into 2-inch chunks
- Herbs of your choosing:
    - tarragon, bay, thyme, rosemary
- 1 rind from a parmesan wedge (optional)
- Water to cover (about 2 cups)

Preparation Method:

1. Combine ingredients in slow cooker, cook on low from five to 24 hours.
2. Remove the veggies in it – use the mesh to strain.
3. Add flavor by adding salt and spice it up with additional pepper.
4. Store in the refrigerator between uses. Yields about 2 cups of stock.

Chapter 1: Heartwarming Breakfasts

A warm, cozy breakfast is always welcome. A warm, cozy breakfast you barely cooked, all ready for you when you wake up? Even better. Below are recipes that you can make in the morning or prep the night before for maximum efficiency. Extra points if you pre-set your coffee maker.

Apple French Toast

Serves 4, 2 hours
This recipe requires night-before prep, and then cooked for two hours in the morning, so save it for a morning where you can relax a bit before breakfast is ready. French toast is recommended, but challah bread does have a wonderfully sweet, honeyed flavor.

Ingredients

- 1 large loaf of French bread or challah, cut to cubes (1-inch)
- 2 cups milk of your choosing
- ¼ cup brown sugar
- 2 tsp. cinnamon
- 4 eggs
- 2 green apples, peeled and cubed, covered in 1 Tbsp. white sugar
- ¼ tsp. nutmeg

Preparation Method:

1. Grease the slow cooker using the cooking spray. Place bread cubes in the bottom of the cooker.

2. Mix eggs, milk, sugar, and spices together in a large bowl. Pour egg mixture over the bread, squishing the bread down to fully submerge if necessary.
3. Place apples on top of bread and egg combination. Put on the lid to close and continue to let it cook on high for 2 hours.
4. Serve topped with maple syrup if desired.

Cinnamon Rolls

Serves 6, 2.5 hours

Time is of the essence, so buying cinnamon rolls from the freezer section will speed up the process without sacrificing flavor.

Ingredients

- 2 12-oz tubes of cinnamon roll dough, divided and cut into quarters, icing reserved
- ½ cup milk
- 1 tsp. cinnamon
- 4 eggs
- 2 tsp. vanilla
- ½ tsp. nutmeg

Preparation Method:

1. Grease your slow cooker using the cooking spray.
2. Layer the cinnamon rolls on the slow cooker, completely covering the bottom.
3. Whisk together milk, eggs, and spices in a separate bowl, pour over cinnamon rolls.
4. Cover the liquid with another layer of cinnamon rolls.
5. Spread icing over the top layer. Put on the lid to close and continue to let it cook on low for 2 ½ hours.

Chocolate Raspberry French Toast

Serves 4, 2 hours
This recipe calls for dark chocolate chips for a rich flavor, but white chocolate will lean into dessert-for-breakfast territory, and milk chocolate will swing sweet as well.

Ingredients

- 1 large loaf of French bread or challah, cut into 1-inch cubes
- 1 tsp. Vanilla
- 4 eggs
- 2 cups milk
- ½ pint raspberries
- ¼ cup white or brown sugar
- ½ cup dark chocolate chips

Preparation Method:

1. Grease all the sides of the slow cooker using a cooking spray.
2. Lay only ½ of the cubed bread in the cooker, then over it lay ½ of the raspberries and chocolate chips, cover with remaining bread and another layer of chocolate chips and raspberries.
3. Mix eggs, vanilla, milk, and sugar in a large bowl.
4. Pour egg mixture over the bread, squishing the bread down to fully submerge if necessary.
5. Put on the lid to close and continue to let it cook on high for 2 hours.

Chai-Spiced Monkey Bread

Serves 8, 2.5 hours

Grab yourself a tube of biscuit rounds from the freezer the next time you go shopping, and make this recipe the next time you're hankering for something cozy and spicy.

Ingredients

- 1 container biscuit rounds
- ½ cup white sugar
- ½ tsp. nutmeg
- ½ brown sugar
- ¼ cup butter – melted
- 2 tsp. cinnamon
- ¼ cup chai tea concentrate

Preparation Method:

1. Grease slow cooker with cooking spray.
2. Cut each biscuit round into six pieces.
3. Put white sugar, brown sugar, and spices into a zip plastic bag.
4. Dip each biscuit piece in melted butter, then place in bag. Once all the biscuits are in the bag, seal the bag and shake to coat.
5. Pour any remaining butter and chai tea concentrate into the slow cooker, then add the sugared biscuits, completely covering the bottom.
6. Cover and let it cook at low for 2 ½ hours.

Orange Sweet Rolls

Serves 8, 2 hours

This is a new take on the cinnamon roll, and the citrus is perfect for summer mornings.

Ingredients

- 1 package crescent dough
- ½ cup brown sugar
- ½ cup butter, softened
- ⅓ cup orange marmalade
- 1 cup powdered sugar
- Zest and juice of 1 orange

Preparation Method:

1. Unroll the crescent dough and spread with softened butter.
2. Spread orange marmalade over butter, sprinkle with brown sugar.
3. Roll the crescent dough into a log and cut into 8 pieces.
4. Spray the bottom and sides of your slow cooker with cooking spray.
5. Place buns in the slow cooker, put on the lid to close and continue to let it cook on high for 2 hours.
6. Mix powdered sugar, zest, and orange juice together (add melted butter if the consistency is too thick).
7. Before serving, glaze orange rolls with juice mixture.

Basic Oatmeal

Serves 6, 8 hours

If you like the convenience of overnight oats but crave the warmth you get from oatmeal, this is for you.

Ingredients

- 1 cup steel cut oats
- 3 ½ cups water

Preparation Method:

1. Place water and oats in the slow cooker.
2. Put on the lid to close and continue to let it cook on low for 8 hours.
3. Top with spices, nuts, or fruit.

Berry Almond Vegan Quinoa

Serves 4, 6 hours

This recipe is completely vegan. Add any toppings you want.

Ingredients

- 1 cup almond milk
- 1 cup water
- 1 cup frozen mixed berries
- 1 cup quinoa
- 1 mashed ripe banana

Preparation Method:

1. Lay all ingredients in slow cooker.
2. Put on the lid to close and continue to let it cook on low for 6 hours.
3. Top with nuts, spices, or fruit.

Meat and Potato Scramble

Serves 4, 8 hours

This is a make-ahead breakfast, and perfect for feeding all those hungry kids after the sleepover!

Ingredients

- 12 eggs
- 1 cup fully cooked sausage links chopped into chunks
- 1 cup water
- 1 bag frozen hash browns or other breakfast cut of potato
- 16 oz. shredded cheddar cheese or cheese of choice (make a mix of cheeses if you'd like)
- 1 cup cooked, chopped bacon

Preparation Method:

1. Grease the sides of slow cooker with cooking spray.
2. Mix the sausage, bacon, potatoes, and cheese together in the slow cooker.
3. Whisk eggs and water in a separate bowl, then mix into the potato mixture in the crockpot.
4. Top with more cheese, making sure that the cheese doesn't hit the sides of the slow cooker (it will burn).
5. Put on the lid to close and continue to let it cook on low for 5-8 hours.
6. Add flavor by adding salt and spice it up with additional pepper.

Southwestern Scramble

Serves 4, 8 hours

This feeds a crowd well, as the toppings allow you to personalize your breakfast experience. Subtract the meat for a vegetarian option.

Ingredients

- 12 eggs
- 1 bag frozen hash browns or other breakfast cut of potato
- 1 cup water
- 16 oz. shredded cheddar cheese or cheese of choice (make a mix of cheeses if you'd like)
- 1 cup fully cooked sausage links chopped into chunks
- 1 can of green chiles, chopped
- Toppings for serving:
    - 1 cup chopped green onions
    - 1 cup chopped tomatoes
    - Salsas or hot sauce of choice
    - Sour cream

Preparation Method:

1. Spray the bottom and sides of slow cooker with cooking spray.
2. Mix the sausage, chiles, potatoes, and cheese together in the slow cooker.
3. Whisk eggs and water in a separate bowl, then mix into the potato mixture in the crockpot.
4. Top with more cheese, making sure that the cheese doesn't hit the sides of the slow cooker (it will burn).
5. Put on the lid to close and continue to let it cook on low for 5-8 hours.
6. Add flavor by adding salt and spice it up with additional pepper. Top with desired items.

Chapter 2: Easy Snacks

If there is anything more stressful than preparing food for a large party, we would like to know about it. Rummaging through the pantry in hopes of finding a spare bag of chips is about as good as snacks for a crowd can get. However, bringing your slow cooker into the mix will unlock not only delicious treats but also save you hours of cooking. That means you can vacuum while your slow cooker works.

Chex Mix

Serves 12, 3 hours
A classic snack made in a simple way. What's not to love?

Ingredients

- 9 cups Chex cereal (can be any type or combination of several types)
- 1 cup peanuts
- 2 cups pretzels
- ⅓ cup butter, melted and still hot
- 1 Tbsp. salt
- 1 cup Cheerios
- ¼ cup Worcester sauce

Preparation Method:

1. Combine butter, salt, and sauce together in the slow cooker, add cereals, pretzels, and peanuts. Mix to combine.
2. Put on the lid to close and continue to let it cook on low for 3 hours, stirring every hour to prevent burning.

Tangy Smokies

Serves 8, 1 hour
This twist on gameday little smokies needs only four ingredients to make this sweet and spicy treat.

Ingredients

- 1 package miniature hot dogs or sausages
- 1 cup ketchup
- 1 tsp. horseradish paste
- 1 Tbsp. brown sugar

Preparation Method:

1. Combine ketchup, horseradish, and brown sugar in the slow cooker, add miniature hot dogs.
2. Mix to cover hot dogs.
3. Put on the lid to close and continue to let it cook on low for 1 hour.

Buffalo Chicken Dip

Serves 10, 2 hours

The smoky, spicy buffalo chicken wing turns into a party dip. Serve with chips, pretzels, or anything handy!

Ingredients

- 3 cups chopped cooked chicken
- 1 package cream cheese, cut into cubes
- 1 cup shredded mozzarella cheese
- ½ tsp. garlic powder
- 1 cup shredded Colby Jack cheese
- 1 cup sour cream
- 1 cup hot sauce
- ½ tsp. onion powder
- ½ cup blue cheese
- ½ tsp. black pepper
- ½ tsp. cayenne pepper

Preparation Method:

1. Combine all the components except for the chicken into the slow cooker, mixing to fully combine.
2. Add chicken and stir.
3. Put on the lid to close and continue to let it cook on low for 2 hours, stirring every hour.

Candied Pecans

Serves 4, 3 hours

Need gift ideas for the holidays? Use any type or combination of nuts in this spicy, sweet classic.

Ingredients

- 4 cups pecans
- 1 egg white
- 1 cup white sugar
- ½ cup brown sugar
- 2 Tbsp. cinnamon
- ¼ cup water
- 2 tsp. vanilla
- 1 tsp. cayenne (optional, for sweet and spicy nuts)

Preparation Method:

1. Mix together sugars and cinnamon.
2. In a separate bowl, whisk together egg white and vanilla until frothy.
3. Spray sides and bottom of slow cooker with cooking spray, add nuts.
4. Add egg mixture to nuts and stir to combine.
5. Sprinkle sugar mixture over nuts, stirring to combine.
6. Put on the lid to close and continue to let it cook on low for 3 hours, stirring every 20 minutes. The last 20 minutes, stir in water.
7. Remove from slow cooker after time is up and allow to cool on a baking sheet.

Corn and Jalapeno Dip

Serves 6, 2 ¼ hours
Southwestern kick and slow cooker tricks.

Ingredients

- 4 slices cooked bacon, cooked and diced
- ½ cup sour cream
- 2 jalapenos, seeded and diced
- 1 cup shredded Pepper Jack cheese
- 3 cans whole kernel corn, drained
- 1 package cream cheese, cubed
- ½ chopped scallions

Preparation Method:

1. Mix corn, jalapenos, sour cream, and cheese together in slow cooker. Top with cream cheese cubes.
2. Put on the lid to close and continue to let it cook on low for 2 hours.
3. Stir cream cheese into dip, put on the lid to close and continue to let it cook on high for 15 minutes.
4. Add flavor by adding salt and spice it up with additional pepper, serve topped with scallions and bacon.

Pumpkin Granola

Serves 8, 2 ½ hours

Seasonal flavors are always a hit, and this pumpkin granola will be an excellent treat to share with friends. Or to keep at home all to yourself.

Ingredients

- 1 cup honey or maple syrup
- 2 tsp. vanilla
- ½ cup pumpkin puree
- ¼ cup vegetable oil
- 1 tsp. cinnamon
- ¼ cup sunflower seeds
- ½ tsp. ginger
- 4 cups steel cut oats
- ¼ tsp. nutmeg
- ¼ tsp. cloves
- 1 cup puffed rice cereal
- ¼ cup pumpkin seeds

Preparation Method:

1. Spray bottom and sides of slow cooker with cooking spray.
2. Combine wet ingredients (puree, honey, oil, vanilla).
3. Combine dry ingredients in a separate bowl, then mix the two bowls together.
4. Place entire mixture in slow cooker. Put on the lid to close and continue to let it cook on low for 2 ½ hours, stirring every 30 minutes.
5. Allow to cool on parchment paper or aluminum foil.

Chapter 3: Tasty Meat Dishes

After a long day at work or running errands, or simply just after a long day, there is nothing more comforting than a meal you barely had to make. Of course, frozen dinners are always an option, but every cardboard box of mix-ins is beat by tender beef roast or tangy pineapple pork.

Some recipes within this section will recommend browning the meat first. This keeps the meat juicy while it's in the slow cooker and adds a wonderful flavor, but it's not necessary. The recipes will work with or without browning; the choice is up to you.

Browning meat

1. Heat 1 Tbsp. oil in a frying pan.
2. Add a dash of salt to all sides of meat and place in pan.
3. When one side has gone dark, about 3 minutes, turn meat to an uncooked side.
4. Remove meat when browned on all sides.
5. For ground sausage, break apart and stir every two minutes until deep brown.

Beef Pot Roast with Vegetables

Serves 8, 8 hours

This hearty meal is perfect for cold nights, but let's face it, it's also perfect for pretending it's a cold night.

Ingredients

- 4 lbs. chuck roast, browned
- 1 Tbsp. onion powder
- 1 yellow onion, skin removed and thinly chopped
- 2 garlic cloves, whole or chopped
- 1 stalk celery, chopped
- 3 Russet or yellow potatoes, cubed (optional peeled)
- 2 carrots, chopped

Preparation Method:

1. Place browned roast and vegetables in the slow cooker with 1 cup of water.
2. Put on the lid to close and continue to let it cook on low for 8 to 10 hours.
3. Add flavor by adding salt and spice it up with additional pepper.

White Bean Chicken Chili

Serves 6, 8 hours

For a less spicy version, switch out the jalapenos for mild green chiles.

Ingredients

- 1 chicken breast, boneless and skinless, browned
- 1 white onion, skin removed and thinly chopped
- 2 garlic cloves
- 1 cup chicken stock
- ½ jalapeno, seeded and chopped
- 1 cup water
- 1 can white cannellini beans or navy beans

Preparation Method:

1. Combine all the components in the slow cooker.
2. Put on the lid to close and continue to let it cook on low for 8 hours.
3. After cooking, shred the chicken using two forks in a crossing motion or use your hands.
4. Add flavor by adding salt and spice it up with additional pepper.
5. Serve with rice and top with cheese, tomatoes, or scallions.

Sausage and Kale Soup

Serves 6, 6 hours

Certain Italian eatery closed? This slow cooker cheat gets you the soup you love in sweatpants.

Ingredients

- 1-pound spicy Italian ground sausage, browned
- 1 garlic clove, cut up
- 4 Russet potatoes, cubed
- 1 white onion, skin removed and thinly chopped
- 3 cups chicken stock
- 2 cups chopped kale (remove stem and tear with hands or chop roughly)
- 2 Tbsp. flour
- 1 cup milk, whipping cream, half-and-half

Preparation Method:

1. Combine first five ingredients in slow cooker, adding water to cover the meat if necessary.
2. Put on the lid to close and continue to let it cook on low for 6 hours.
3. Half an hour before serving, stir in flour until it dissolved completely.
4. Add cream and kale, cook on high for 30 minutes.
5. Add flavor by adding salt and spice it up with additional pepper, add cayenne to taste if desired.

Lemon Herb Chicken

Serves 4, 8 hours

Fresh or dried herbs will work equally well in this powerful, Mediterranean-inspired dish.

Ingredients

- 1 chicken breast, boneless and skinless, browned
- 1 yellow onion, skin removed and thinly chopped
- ½ tsp. rosemary
- 2 garlic cloves, cut up
- ½ tsp. oregano
- ½ tsp. thyme
- ½ lemon, juiced (reserved) and cut into slices

Preparation Method:

1. Mix lemon juice with 1 cup water in slow cooker.
2. Add chicken, onion, garlic, and spices. Place lemon slices on top of chicken breast.
3. Put on the lid to close and continue to let it cook on low for 8 hours.
4. Add flavor by adding salt and spice it up with additional pepper.

Moroccan-Spiced Lamb

Serves 6, 6 hours

The complex flavors you thought included a plane ticket? Think again. Bring the sweet/sour/spicy flavors of Morocco to the ease of a slow cooker.

Ingredients

- 2 lbs. lamb stew meat or lamb shoulder cut into 1-inch cubes
- 1 yellow onion, skin removed and thinly chopped
- ¼ tsp. cinnamon
- 3 garlic cloves, cut up
- 1 Tbsp. ginger
- 1 Tbsp. cumin
- ¼ tsp. cayenne
- 1 can diced tomatoes, not drained
- 2 tsp. coriander
- 1 can chickpeas, rinsed and drained
- ¼ cup dried apricots or raisins

Preparation Method:

1. Brown lamb meat in oil, adding onion, garlic, spices, and tomatoes the last minute.
2. Once onion is soft, transfer all ingredients to slow cooker, including chickpeas and apricots.
3. Put on the lid to close and continue to let it cook on low for 6 hours.
4. Add flavor by adding salt and spice it up with additional pepper.
5. Serve over rice or couscous with a dollop of plain yogurt and chopped mint.

Pineapple Pork

Serves 6, 8 hours

Four ingredient recipes make for a low-hassle evening. This recipe is so simple that you can include the kids in the making process.

Ingredients

- 1 pork butt
- 1 can pineapple chunks, drained
- 1 white onion, peeled and quartered
- 2 cups teriyaki sauce

Preparation Method:

1. Combine all the components in the slow cooker with ½ cup water or beef broth.
2. Put on the lid to close and continue to let it cook on low for 8 hours.
3. Add flavor by adding salt and spice it up with additional pepper.

Chicken Stir Fry

Serves 4, 8 hours

No wok? No problem! The ingredients get a char from a quick fry, then soften in a slow cooker. The vegetables you add are up to you.

Ingredients

- ½ cup soy sauce
- 1 Tbsp. rice vinegar or apple cider vinegar
- 1 Tbsp. honey or similar sweetener
- 1 chicken breast, boneless and skinless, browned
- 1 yellow onion, peeled and cut into strips
- 1 cup sliced mushrooms
- 1 bell pepper, cut into strips
- 1 zucchini, cut into chunks
- 1 garlic clove, cut up
- 1 cup sliced cabbage
- 1 cup broccoli chunks

Preparation Method:

1. Combine first four ingredients in slow cooker.
2. Once combined, add all the other ingredients to the slow cooker, putting the vegetables that need to cook longest (like onions and squashes) on the bottom.
3. Add ½ cup water. Put on the lid to close and continue to let it cook on low for 8 hours.
4. Add flavor by adding salt and spice it up with additional pepper

Spaghetti Sauce

Serves 6, 8 hours

Homemade spaghetti sauce trumps store bought any time. Eliminate the tinned-can taste, add any spices you want, and enjoy over the pasta of your choice or use as a dipping sauce.

Ingredients

- 1-pound spicy Italian ground sausage
- 1-pound ground beef
- 1 white onion, skin removed and thinly chopped
- 2 garlic cloves, cut up
- ½ tsp. oregano
- 2 bay leaves
- ½ tsp. rosemary
- ½ tsp. basil
- ½ tsp. thyme
- ¾ cup tomato paste
- 3 cans diced tomatoes

Preparation Method:

1. Combine tomato paste and juice from canned tomatoes with 1 cup water in slow cooker.
2. Brown meats with onion and garlic.
3. Combine all the components in the slow cooker, placing bay leaves on top for easy removal later.
4. Put on the lid to close and continue to let it cook on low for 8 hours.
5. Add flavor by adding salt and spice it up with additional pepper.

Whole Turkey

Serves 8, 8 hours

This recipe not only promises to cook a whole turkey in your slow cooker (freeing up the oven for other holiday matters) but also includes quick recipes for stuffing and gravy incorporating the ingredients used in cooking the turkey. The result? A holiday meal for 8 from one slow cooker.

Ingredients

- 1 Tbsp. salt
- 2 tsp. Paprika
- 2 tsp. thyme
- 1 tsp. onion powder
- 2 tsp. ground black pepper
- 8 to 9-lb turkey, organs removed
- ½ white onion, skin removed and thinly chopped
- 1 celery stalk, chopped
- 4 garlic cloves, cut up
- 1 carrot, chopped
- 1 lemon, quartered

Preparation Method:

1. Combine spices and rub on the inside and outside of turkey.
2. Place lemon and one garlic clove in the body cavity, tie turkey legs with twine.
3. Place vegetables on the bottom if the slow cooker, cover with turkey.
4. Put on the lid to close and continue to let it cook on low for 6-8 hours.
5. Remove from slow cooker and transfer turkey to an oven-safe dish.

6. Broil in oven for 3 minutes, watching to make sure the turkey doesn't burn.
7. Rest the turkey for 30 minutes before slicing and serving.

Stuffing

1. Roughly chop vegetables from slow cooker.
2. Add flavor by adding salt and spice it up with additional pepper.
3. Combine with browned Italian sausage and 8 cups torn cornbread or baguette.
4. Add to greased 9x13" baking dish, pour 1 cup chicken stock over mixture.
5. Cover dish with foil and bake at 350F for 30 minutes, uncover foil and bake for an additional 15 minutes.

Gravy

1. Brown turkey organs or gizzard from turkey to 1 Tbsp. oil and brown with salt.
2. Remove meat pieces; add ¼ cup turkey juices from slow cooker until combined.
3. Add 1 Tbsp. unsalted butter, stir to combine.
4. Add 1 Tbsp. flour, stirring quickly to combine.
5. Add spoonfuls of flour until desired consistency.
6. Add flavor by adding salt and spice it up with additional pepper.

Chapter 4: Vegetarian and Delicious

While slow cookers evoke images of braised meats, there is no reason that meatless dishes can't have their day. Vegetables can find the same tenderness and flavor that meats can in slow cooking recipes. Slow cooking, in fact, brings out the savory elements in veggies dishes, lending those tastes usually found in pork or beef. Use these vegetarian and vegan slow cooker recipes and enjoy the delicious aspects of vegetables often overlooked.

Teriyaki Tofu

Serves 6, 4 hours
Firm tofu has a similar texture to meats, but this dish is entirely plant-based.

Ingredients

- 1-pound firm tofu, browned and cut into cubes
- 1 Tbsp. honey
- 1 Tbsp. ginger
- ¼ cup orange juice or grapefruit juice
- ¼ soy sauce

Preparation Method:

1. Combine all but the tofu in the slow cooker, mixing thoroughly.
2. Add tofu to slow cooker.
3. Put on the lid to close and continue to let it cook on low for 4 hours.
4. Add flavor by adding salt and spice it up with additional pepper.

Southwestern Chowder

Serves 6, 6 hours

Corn and potatoes beef up this spicy chowder.

Ingredients

- 1 white onion, skin removed and thinly chopped
- ½ jalapeno, seeded and chopped
- 2 garlic cloves
- 1 cup vegetable stock
- 1 cup water
- 1 can white cannellini beans or navy beans
- 1 cup corn
- 3 Russet potatoes, cubed

Preparation Method:

1. Combine all the components in the slow cooker.
2. Put on the lid to close and continue to let it cook on low for 6 hours.
3. Add flavor by adding salt and spice it up with additional pepper.

Chickpea Tagine

Serves 6, 6 hours

Tagine is a method used in Africa and the Middle East to braise. This recipe utilizes the same idea to braise whole chickpeas slowly. They come out soft and flavorful.

Ingredients

- 2 Tbsp. flour
- 1 yellow onion, skin removed and thinly chopped
- 4 garlic cloves, cut up
- 1 Tbsp. ginger
- 2 Tbsp. tomato paste
- 2 cans chopped tomatoes
- 3 Tbsp. honey
- 1 cup vegetable stock
- 1 tsp. coriander
- 1 tsp. cayenne
- 2 cans chickpeas
- 1 tsp. Cinnamon
- 2 cans chickpeas
- 1 tsp. cumin
- ½ cup dried apricots

Preparation Method:

1. Saute garlic and onion for 5 minutes, then add flour and chicken stock, stir until smooth. Add all other ingredients except for apricots and chickpeas and saute for another 2 minutes.
2. Combine all the components in the slow cooker. Put on the lid to close and continue to let it cook on low for 6 hours.
3. Add flavor by adding salt and spice it up with additional pepper.

Lo Mein

Serves 6, 4 hours

The beauty of lo mein or other vegetable-centered dishes is the freedom to personalize your veggie choices. Add mushrooms, water chestnuts, green beans, or whatever else you would enjoy.

Ingredients

- ⅓ cup soy sauce
- 3 cloves garlic, cut up
- 2 Tbsp. brown sugar
- 1 tsp. sesame oil
- 3 cups broccoli florets
- 1 carrot, cut into slices
- 1 Tbsp. ginger
- ½ bell pepper, cut into slices
- 1 celery stalk, cut into slices
- 1 cup snow peas
- 1-pound spaghetti or other long noodle

Preparation Method:

1. Combine soy, garlic, brown sugar, ginger, and oil in slow cooker.
2. Add vegetables. Put on the lid to close and continue to let it cook on low for 4 hours.
3. Cook pasta according to package directions.
4. Stir pasta into vegetable mixture. Add flavor by adding salt and spice it up with additional pepper.

Fajita Veggies

Serves 4, 3 hours

These veggies have a similar smoky taste as grilled veggies. Use them as a main dish in tortillas with cheese, or use them as a side dish.

Ingredients

- 2 white onions, peeled and chopped up
- 2 Tbsp. oil
- 2 tsp. hot chili powder
- 6 bell peppers, cut into strips
- 2 tsp. smoked paprika
- 1 tsp. coriander
- 2 cups cherry tomatoes, halved

Preparation Method:

1. Mix the first six ingredients in the slow cooker.
2. Put on the lid to close and continue to let it cook on low for two hours.
3. Stir in tomatoes, and then put on the lid to close and continue to let it cook on low for an additional hour.
4. Add flavor by adding salt and spice it up with additional pepper.

Veggie Pot Pie

Serves 6, 6 hours

A beautiful pot pie is a labor of love and so comforting to the soul. This pot pie, while still comforting, is much less labor, and much more love.

Ingredients

- 2 cups vegetable stock
- 2 Tbsp. cornstarch or flour
- 1-pound Russet potatoes, skin removed and chopped into dice
- 1 medium yellow onion, diced
- 1 tsp. thyme
- 3 medium carrots, skin-removed and chopped into dice
- 2 medium stalks celery, diced
- 2 cloves garlic, cut up
- 1 Tbsp. apple cider vinegar
- 2 bay leaves
- 1 tsp. kosher salt
- 1/4 tsp. freshly ground black pepper
- ½ cup heavy cream
- 1 tube frozen biscuits
- 1 cup frozen peas

Preparation Method:

1. Spray sides and bottom of slow cooker with cooking spray.
2. Whisk ½ cup vegetable stock and cornstarch in small bowl until fully combined.
3. Place all spices and vegetables except peas in the slow cooker with remaining stock; add cornstarch mixture until fully combined.

4. Put on the lid to close and continue to let it cook on low for 6 hours.
5. The last 30 minutes, add peas, cream, and vinegar. Make biscuits according to package directions.
6. Salt and pepper vegetable mixture to taste. Serve topped with a biscuit.

Basic Risotto

Serves 6, 4 hours

This is a very basic risotto recipe, and ripe for add-ins. Consider classic additions such as cooked mushrooms, asparagus, or butternut squash. Or, choose your own ingredients to add the last 15 minutes.

Ingredients

- 3 ¾ cups vegetable stock
- 1 ¼ cups arborio rice
- 1 cup Parmesan cheese
- ¼ cup white wine
- 2 cloves garlic, cut up
- ¼ cup olive oil
- 1 shallot, peeled and cut up
- ¼ tsp. black pepper

Preparation Method:

1. Saute garlic and shallot in 1 tsp. olive oil, about three minutes.
2. Pour in white wine (will sizzle and pop).
3. Pour wine and shallot mixture in slow cooker, add rice, stock, olive oil, and pepper.
4. Put on the lid to close and continue to let it cook on low for 4 hours.
5. Stir in Parmesan, cook uncovered on high for 15 minutes.
6. Add flavor by adding salt and spice it up with additional pepper.

Minestrone

Serves 8, 6 hours

A nice crusty bread, a glass of red wine, choosing accompaniments for this soup will be no problem. Exercising patience while it cooks, on the other hand...

Ingredients

- 6 cups vegetable broth
- 1 can crushed tomatoes
- 1 can kidney beans, drained
- 1 white onion, skin removed and thinly chopped
- 1 tsp. thyme
- 2 celery stalks, diced
- 2 tsp. dried oregano
- 2 carrots, diced
- 1 small zucchini
- 3 cloves garlic, cut up
- 1 Tbsp. cut up fresh parsley
- 1 tsp. salt
- 1/2 cup elbow macaroni
- 4 cups chopped fresh spinach

Preparation Method:

1. Combine all the components in slow cooker except for spinach, and macaroni.
2. Put on the lid to close and continue to let it cook on low for 6 hours.
3. Cook macaroni according to package directions.
4. Stir spinach and macaroni into the slow cooker, put on the lid to close and continue to let it cook for another 15 minutes.

5. Top with Parmesan, add flavor by adding salt and spice it up with additional pepper.

African Peanut Stew

Serves 8, 8 hours

Though the combination of ingredients may be strange, the result is perfection. Spicy and a little sweet, this veggie-heavy stew will satisfy even the strongest of carnivores.

Ingredients

- 1 white onion, skin removed and thinly chopped
- 2 red bell peppers, cut into slices
- 4 cloves garlic, cut up
- 1 can crushed tomatoes
- 2 sweet potatoes, peeled and cut into bite-size pieces
- 3 cups sliced carrots
- 4 cups vegetable broth
- ¼ tsp. ground cinnamon
- ½ tsp. curry powder
- ½ tsp. cumin
- ¼ tsp. ground black pepper
- ¼ tsp. cayenne pepper
- ¼ tsp. crushed red pepper flakes
- ¼ tsp. chili powder
- 1 cup brown rice
- 1 cup crunchy peanut butter

Preparation Method:

1. Saute onion, bell peppers, and garlic in 1 Tbsp. oil for five minutes, add to slow cooker.

2. Add all ingredients to slow cooker except for rice and peanut butter.
3. Put on the lid to close and continue to let it cook on low for 5 hours.
4. Add rice, put on the lid to close and continue to let it cook on low for 2 hours.
5. Stir in peanut butter, put on the lid to close and continue to let it cook for another 1 hour.
6. Add flavor by adding salt and spice it up with additional pepper.

Chapter 5: Satisfying Seafood

Seafood isn't too fancy to get the slow cooker treatment. In fact, the gentle heat of a slow cooker is the perfect cooking method for delicate, flaky fish. From fish soups to seafood boils, your slow cooker will be your new best friend when it comes to creatures of the sea. Not a fan of fish? Remove the meat or substitute cooked chicken in each recipe as alternatives.

Shrimp Paella

Serves 6, 4 hours
This recipe mimics the crispy outside, rich inside rich dish, but with typical slow cooker ease. Add 1 l cup each of mussels and scallops to enhance the taste of the shrimp further.

Ingredients

- 3 links chorizo or chicken sausage, browned and cut into slices
- 1 medium onion, chopped
- 1½ cups (dry) long grain brown rice
- 1½ cups chicken stock
- 1 tsp. ground turmeric
- ½ cup fennel, chopped
- 1 medium bell pepper, chopped
- 2 cups diced canned tomatoes
- ½ tsp. ground paprika
- 1 cup peeled, deveined shrimp, tails on or off

Preparation Method:

1. Combine all the components except for the shrimp (or other seafood) in the slow cooker.

2. Put on the lid to close and continue to let it cook on low for 3 ½ hours.
3. Add shrimp, stirring to combine, put on the lid to close, and continue to let it cook on low for another 30 minutes.
4. Add flavor by adding salt and spice it up with additional pepper.

Clam Chowder

Serves 4, 7 hours

A day at the beach, replicated in the kitchen. Sandy shoes optional.

Ingredients

- ½ white onion, skin removed and thinly chopped
- 1 garlic clove, cut up
- ½ tsp. thyme
- 1 cup water
- 1 cup corn
- 1 cup chicken stock
- 2 stalks celery, chopped
- 2 Russet potatoes, cubed
- 1 tsp. lemon juice
- 2 cups clam (fresh, canned, or frozen), cut into strips
- 2 strips bacon, cooked and chopped
- 1 cup cream
- 1 tsp. cornstarch

Preparation Method:

1. Combine first eight ingredients in slow cooker.
2. Put on the lid to close and continue to let it cook on low for 6 ½ hours.
3. In a separate bowl, combine cream and cornstarch, whisking until smooth, then add to slow cooker.
4. Add remaining ingredients. Put on the lid to close and continue to let it cook on low for another 30 minutes.
5. Add flavor by adding salt and spice it up with additional pepper.

Scallop Risotto

Serves 6, 4 hours

Though most recipes in this book allow browning to be optional, browning the scallops before adding them to the slow cooker is highly recommended. They will have a much more pleasing texture, and the caramelized bits on the surface will flavor the risotto.

Ingredients

- 1 cup small scallops, browned, or 6 large scallops, browned
- 3 ¾ cups vegetable stock
- 1 ¼ cups arborio rice
- ¼ cup olive oil
- 2 cloves garlic, cut up
- 1 shallot, peeled and cut up
- ¼ cup white wine
- ¼ tsp. black pepper

Preparation Method:

1. Saute garlic and shallot in 1 tsp. olive oil, about three minutes.
2. Pour in white wine (will sizzle and pop).
3. Pour wine and shallot mixture in slow cooker, add rice, stock, olive oil, and pepper.
4. Put on the lid to close and continue to let it cook on low for 2 hours.
5. Stir in scallops, put on the lid to close and continue to let it cook on low for another 2 hours.
6. Add flavor by adding salt and spice it up with additional pepper.

Maple Salmon

Serves 4, 4 hours

This classic Northwest dish, usually grilled, goes easy with a slow cooker. The sweet and sour glaze enhances the flavor of the salmon and transports you to the lush forests of Oregon without the cost of airfare.

Ingredients

- 4 salmon fillets (fresh or frozen, defrosted)
- ¼ cup soy sauce
- ½ cup maple syrup (real is the best)
- 2 Tbsp. lime juice
- 1 tsp. ginger
- 1 Tbsp. sesame oil or other oil

Preparation Method:

1. Combine oil, syrup, lime, soy, and ginger in the slow cooker, stirring to combine.
2. Add salmon. Put on the lid to close and continue to let it cook on low for 4 hours.
3. Add flavor by adding salt and spice it up with additional pepper.

Lobster Bisque

Serves 6, 7 hours

This romantic dish is easier to love with this slow cooker hack. Lobster may seem intimidating, but this recipe makes it easy and the payoff will be extraordinary.

Ingredients

- 2 shallots, finely cut up
- 1 clove garlic, finely cut up
- 1 Tbsp. Old Bay Seasoning
- 1 tsp. dried dill
- 2 cups water
- ¼ cup fresh parsley, chopped
- ½ tsp. Paprika
- 2 cans petite diced tomatoes
- 4 lobster tails
- 2 cups chicken stock
- 2 cups heavy cream

Preparation Method:

1. Saute shallots and garlic in 1 Tbsp. oil until soft, about 3 minutes.
2. Add tomatoes, spices, water, and stock to slow cooker.
3. Remove fan part of lobster tails with a sharp knife; add to slow cooker.
4. Put on the lid to close and continue to let it cook on low for 6 hours.
5. Discard lobster tail ends. Blend soup mixture to desired texture and return mixture to slow cooker.
6. Add lobster tails, put on the lid to close and continue to let it cook on low for 1 hour.
7. Remove tails and add cream to soup, stirring to combine.

8. With a sharp knife cut each lobster tail in half long-ways and remove the lobster flesh from the shells.
9. Discard shells and roughly chop lobster meat and add back into the soup. Add flavor by adding salt and spice it up with additional pepper.

Cioppino

Serves 4, 7 hours

An Italian seafood stew, cioppino (pronounced chih-pee-noh) combines the sweet-salty meatiness of different seafoods with the tang of tomatoes and the heat of various spices. It truly is the perfect dish.

Ingredients

- 1 white onion, skin removed and chopped into dice
- 10 garlic cloves, cut into slices
- 1 cup dry white wine
- 2 tsp. tomato paste
- 2 cups water
- 2 Tbsp. oregano
- 2 Tbsp. thyme
- 1 tsp. crushed red pepper
- 2 cups chopped fresh tomatoes
- 1-pound cod, cut into 2-inch pieces
- ½ pound sea scallops
- 1 cup fennel, chopped
- ½ pound shrimp, peeled and deveined
- 1 Tbsp. fresh lemon juice
- 2 bay leaves
- 1/4 cup fresh basil leaves

Preparation Method:

1. Saute onion, fennel, and garlic in 1 Tbsp. oil for 4 minutes.
2. Add wine and tomato paste to pan, stirring to combine.
3. Add to slow cooker. Add water and spices, put on the lid to close and continue to let it cook on low for 7 hours. Add cod, scallops, shrimp, and lemon juice. Put on the lid to close and continue to let it cook on low for 15 minutes.

4. Add flavor by adding salt and spice it up with additional pepper.

Shrimp Boil

Serves 6, 6 hours

A shrimp boil is cause for celebration in Southern states and can be just as celebrated anywhere in the world. Serve this dish on a table covered in butcher paper for authenticity, and let everyone eat with their hands!

Ingredients

- 1 lb. small red potatoes (cut in half)
- 4 cups of water
- 1 white onion, peeled and quartered
- 1 bottle (12 oz) beer or 1 ½ cups chicken stock
- ¼ cup Old Bay Seasoning
- 1 stalk celery, cut into 1-inch pieces
- 2 lemons, cut in half
- 1 lb. cooked kielbasa sausage, cut into 1-inch pieces
- 4 fresh cobs of corn, cut into 3-inch chunks
- 4 garlic cloves, cut up
- 2 lbs. fresh, uncooked large shrimp in shells

Preparation Method:

1. Coat slow cooker with cooking spray.
2. Combine Old Bay, garlic, water, and beer in the slow cooker, stirring to combine.
3. Add vegetables and lemons to slow cooker. Put on the lid to close and continue to let it cook on low for 4 hours.
4. Add sausage, shrimp, and corn, put on the lid to close and continue to let it cook for another 2 hours.

5. Drain liquid through a strainer.
6. Add flavor by adding salt and spice it up with additional pepper.

Chapter 6: Cozy Desserts

Perhaps you want to create a dinner from scratch. Use your slow cooker instead to make a delicious dessert; just push "on" while you're preparing dinner and it will be done by the time the kids go to bed. If you can wait that long. The smell of a sweet treat may overtake whatever you're cooking.

Blackberry Cobbler

Serves 6, 8 hours

This recipe includes a little elbow grease with making the dumpling dough, but the result is buttery dumplings perched atop tangy, sweet berries. Any berry or combination of berry can be substituted. Serve with vanilla ice cream for maximum pleasure.

Ingredients

- 5 cups fresh or frozen blackberries
- 1 cup sugar
- ¼ cup butter, melted
- 2 Tbsp. cornstarch
- 1 tsp. baking powder
- 2 cups all-purpose flour
- ¼ cup milk
- ½ tsp. salt

Preparation Method:

1. Spray the sides and bottom of slow cooker with cooking spray.
2. Combine ½ cup sugar, berries, and cornstarch in the slow cooker.

3. In another bowl or mixer, combine flour, ½ cup sugar, butter, milk, baking powder, and salt until it forms a soft dough.
4. Drop the batter by the spoonful on the berry mixture, leaving space between dumplings and avoiding sides of the slow cooker.
5. Put on the lid to close and continue to let it cook on low for 8 hours.

Lemon Poppyseed Cake

Serves 6

Yes, cake! This recipe will be perfect for the days when the oven is otherwise occupied.

Ingredients

- 12 Tbsp. unsalted butter, at room temperature
- 2 large eggs
- 1 cup sour cream
- 1 tsp. baking soda
- ½ tsp. pure vanilla extract
- 1 ¾ cups all-purpose flour
- 1 tsp. baking powder
- ¼ tsp. kosher salt
- Zest and juice from ½ lemon
- 1 ¼ cups granulated sugar
- 1 Tbsp. poppy seeds

Preparation Method:

1. In a large mixing bowl, beat together the butter, eggs, and 1 ¼ cups of granulated sugar until creamy. Mix in sour cream, vanilla, lemon zest, and poppy seeds.
2. In a separate medium bowl, whisk together the flour, baking powder, baking soda, and salt. Slowly add to the wet ingredients and mix on low until combined.
3. Line the bottom and sides of the bowl of a slow cooker with parchment paper. Pour the batter into the lined slow cooker bowl. Put on the lid to close and continue to let it cook on high for 2 ½ hours, or until a toothpick inserted into the center comes out clean.
4. Combine the lemon juice and another 6 Tbsp. granulated sugar in a small bowl.

5. Drizzle over baked cake in the slow cooker.
6. Grab the parchment paper and lift the cake out of the slow cooker. Transfer to a wire rack to cool for 15 minutes before serving.

Baked Apples

Serves 4, 6 hours
This classic recipe is great served with ice cream or cook overnight for morning oatmeal.

Ingredients

- 4 apples, cored and peeled
- ½ cup water
- ½ tsp. allspice or clove
- 8 Tbsp. brown sugar
- 2 tsp. cinnamon
- 4 Tbsp. butter

Preparation Method:

1. Combine brown sugar and spices in separate bowl.
2. Place apples in slow cooker and fill with sugar mixture, pushing mixture firmly into apple.
3. Top each apple with 1 Tbsp. butter.
4. Add water to the bottom of slow cooker.
5. Put on the lid to close and continue to let it cook on low for 6 hours.

Cheesecake

Serves 12, 10 hours

Cheesecake for a crowd is a daunting idea, but making it in a slow cooker removes the pressure. Serve with berries.

Ingredients

- 1 ½ cups graham cracker crumbs
- 5 large eggs
- 6 Tbsp. melted butter
- 1 Tbsp. vanilla
- 24 ounces cream cheese
- 1 ½ cups sour cream
- 1 ¼ cups granulated sugar
- 3 Tbsp. all-purpose flour
- ½ tsp. salt

Preparation Method:

1. Line slow cooker with parchment paper, coat with cooking spray.
2. Place the graham crackers in the food processor and pulse into crumbs.
3. Add butter and pulse to combine.
4. Pour the crumbs into the crock and press evenly over the bottom.
5. Mix remaining ingredients until smooth and fully combined.
6. Pour filling over the crust.
7. Put on the lid to close and continue to let it cook on low for 7 hours.
8. Wipe the moisture off the lid and move to refrigerator to chill for 3 hours.
9. Carefully lift the entire cheesecake out of the slow cooker by the edges of the paper.

Rice Pudding

Serves 8, 7 hours

The sticky sweet simplicity of rice pudding makes this recipe a classic.

Ingredients

- 4 cups milk
- 1/2 tsp. vanilla extract
  ½ cup white sugar
- 1 Tbsp. butter
  1/2 cup long-grain white rice
- 1/2 tsp. almond extract
- 1/8 tsp. salt

Preparation Method:

1. Combine all the components in the slow cooker.
2. Put on the lid to close and continue to let it cook on low for 6 hours.
3. Transfer pudding to a glass baking dish, cover with plastic wrap leaving two corners uncovered to vent and refrigerate for 1 hour.

Hot Chocolate

Serves 10, 2 ½ hours
Drinkable desserts are just as valid, and just as tasty, in a slow cooker.

Ingredients

- 2 oz. unsweetened chocolate, chopped
- 7 oz sweetened condensed milk
- 4 cups milk
- ½ Tbsp. vanilla
- ½ cup semisweet chocolate chips

Preparation Method:

1. Combine chocolates and condensed milk in the slow cooker, put on the lid to close and continue to let it cook on high for 30 minutes and stirring often.
2. Add milk and vanilla, whisking to combine completely.
3. Put on the lid to close and continue to let it cook on low for 2 hours.

Hot Toddy

Serves 10, 30 minutes

This boozy beverage gets its warming touch from nutmeg and its kick from whiskey. Serve straight from the slow cooker.

Ingredients

- 1-quart water
- 1 lemon, thinly cut into slices
- ½ cup turbinado sugar
- 2 ½ cups Scotch whiskey
- ¼ tsp. nutmeg

Preparation Method:

1. Combine lemon, sugar, and water in slow cooker.
2. Put on the lid to close and continue to let it cook on high for 30 minutes, stirring often.
3. Add nutmeg and Scotch, stir to combine.

BONUS:

As a way of saying thank you for purchasing my book, please use your link below to claim your 3 FREE Cookbooks on Health, Fitness & Dieting Instantly

https://bit.ly/2MLwfjP

You can also share your link with your friends and families whom you think that can benefit from the cookbooks or you can forward them the link as a gift!

Printed in Great Britain
by Amazon

68292245R00040